THE
LIFE AND
DEATH OF
A POOL

JOHN STRUTHERS

Copyright © 1993 by John Struthers

First published in the UK in 1993
by Swan Hill Press an imprint of Airlife Publishing Ltd.

British Library Cataloguing in Publication Data
A catalogue record for this book
is available from the British Library

ISBN 1 85310 403 5

Printed by Kyodo Printing Co. (S'pore) Pte Ltd.

Swan Hill Press
an imprint of Airlife Publishing Ltd.
101 Longden Road, Shrewsbury SY3 9EB

Guineafowl moved away from the water's edge as I drew near . . .

Comment

AFRICA IS A CONTINENT, huge and ancient: its abundant diversity of life is a product of both its size and its age. Different species co-inhabit different areas and, where man by the sheer weight of his numbers has not usurped nature, some of these animal species may yet be seen. And the best place to observe them is at a pool.

Water is the blood of life, and nowhere is this more true than in Africa. All over this continent there are pools, natural depressions gathering the summer's rainfall and holding it until rain comes again next season – or as long as they can. These are the gathering places, where Africa's wildlife in all its variety takes turns at quenching its thirst, the inevitable product of day after day of cloudless skies and scorching heat. Winter in Africa is not cold, as it is in the northern hemisphere. There are few places on the continent where one ever sees snow. When drought comes, or at the end of the rainy season, pools dry up. Then, in their desperate need for sustenance, the animals will even drink mud.

This photographer spent six weeks during the heat of an African 'spring season' – September and October – beside a particular pool. That it was called Chine Pool, pronounced Chinhe, is of no great consequence. More important .is the drama I came to observe, one that is re-enacted wherever animals gather in search of this life-giving substance called water.

Whenever a pool fails, that drama is heightened. And most of them do, before summer's rains relieve the animals from thirst's jeopardy. If the rains are delayed, or don't arrive at all, then many animals die. Even a lesser rainfall, a 'light season', increases the pressure during the following winter. This was the case, during the time of my vigil beside Chine Pool.

Chine Pool does not dry up every year, as do many. So the situation I observed was the more poignant. When this usually reliable body of water failed, the many animals that had come to depend upon it had nowhere else nearby to go. Returning each day, eventually every second or third day towards the end, coming to sit beside the waters edge, I became – for a short while – a part of the situation, one with the life of the pool: all of this drove the tragedy home. It was intensely moving to witness the ever-increasing plight of the animals as the days went by and still the rains did not come.

I made no attempt at concealment. Walking each time several kilometres to and from the pool, I selected a shady place – usually with the silhouette broken – and I would settle in. Once the troop of baboons that foraged daily in the vicinity and fed upon the pool's weeds had come to accept me – if not as one of their kind, at least as something not too dissimilar – then the other animal species became less afraid of the human presence too. At one time or another individuals of most species drank within ten metres of where I sat. And, in order to facilitate this growing acceptance, I ended up sitting in the same place each day, shifting position only slightly with the passage of the sun.

I hope the photographs bear witness to the drama – and splendour – of the life of the pool. With words, now, I will try to describe what it was like to be there.

John Struthers

Finally, she began to detour around the fallen tree, and the little one was clearly visible.

MY FIRST CLOSE ENCOUNTER with a wild animal at Chine Pool was very nearly my last. Heading out from the parked vehicle that morning, I'd struck south in the general direction of the pool, but bore a little too far to the left. When, finally, I saw the much reduced, weed-covered body of water, it was at about two o'clock: that is, south-east. Not wanting to disturb the animals in the vicinity any more than was necessary, I decided to continue into the mopani country, then work through it to the pool's edge.

I confess, it was nerve-wracking! Every sound added to the tension of already taut nerves. A troop of baboons, foraging, barred the way; resting on my haunches, I waited for them to move on. That they hadn't spotted me was, I suppose, a tribute to the care I was taking. But finally, gently, I revealed myself, so as to speed their departure; this was taking too long, and I wanted to be settled in beside the pool.

Impalas, too, moved through the dry brush and, ahead, I heard the cracking of branches, indicating an elephant's progress. Now I was almost there. Disturbing only those animals close to the nearer, eastern end of the long pool, I eased out into the open and selected what seemed a good place for the job. Gratefully, I sank into it.

I had chosen a large fallen tree with a main branch that allowed me to rest my back into the vee formed by the junction of the trunk and the branch and so rest the camera, to left or right, just at the ideal height. The near side of the pool was perhaps twenty metres ahead and below, and that would, I thought, allow me to photograph animals drinking on either side of the narrow strip of mud, weed and water.

It wasn't too long before the action started. I'd wiped the sweat from my brow, drunk a few mouthfuls of lukewarm water from a plastic bottle, and begun to watch the impalas drawing nearer,

. . . at a run, exploded over the rise.

when I realised the elephants I had heard earlier were already at the pool. Loud splashing told me they were behind the bush concealing that area of the pool to the left; this was not such a good vantage point, after all. Then I saw them: a young cow, with a small – a very small – calf, accompanied by a teenager. Still bathing, they were moving in my direction; and they were, of course, on 'my' side of the pool.

Seething with excitement, I trained the camera, waiting for the baby to appear from behind its mother's bulk. Directly below me, this young lady now decided to depart the pool, angling up the slope.

Still, the calf was behind her, and I couldn't take the photograph. With every step she took, I was zooming the 28–135mm lens back – and she was coming still closer, trailed by her infant and the teenager. Finally, she began to detour around the fallen tree, and the little one was clearly visible. I took the picture.

But I had left it too late. She came on, and belatedly I realised just what a dangerous situation this was. Too late to move, to stand up, even – but

it was time to let her know I was there: begin talking, at least.

'Hello, girlie,' I said softly. 'It's time to take your baby away, now.'

She stopped; and her ears flared wide as she looked down, little eyes bright. Four elephant paces, I estimated silently, then spoke again.

'It's all right. You can carry on, now,' I said, still softly, trying to keep the tremble out of my voice.

She stood motionless, while the calf walked up behind her. And then, just as the baby elephant reached her side, the young mother took a few paces on past me.

'If the calf had moved in front . . .'.

I dared not move my head as the cow passed, behind me now, for the baby and teenager were still unaware of my presence. Then the cow took my scent. Hearing her reaction, I turned: trunk and tail curling, she was accelerating rapidly, climbing to the top of the rise.

The teenager, leaving the calf in her wake, rushed after. Though my hands were trembling violently by now, I managed a second picture . . . but only because I jammed the body of the camera down on top of the log! Then I nearly dropped it, afterwards, trying to set it down.

Quite definitely, I had chosen too dangerous a place. As soon as the elephants had moved off beyond hearing distance, I gathered up the cameras and carry bag and, impalas or no, skirted the pool to pick a place on the far – more open – side. It took me quite a while to quieten down inside, but by then the animals were approaching the water once more.

I couldn't believe how dry the place was. I had been told that, in May, it was already drier than it had been in the previous October. There was hardly a blade of grass to be seen. Yet the animals were everywhere, and in abundance. How could they survive? The answer was: much longer, and some would not.

The pool was located at a natural boundary between flat, acacia floodplain and the higher mopani/jesse scrubland to the south of it. When, looking eastward, I saw a cloud of dust in the distance heralding the arrival of a large herd of impalas, the beauty of the scene quite took my breath away. And when, later in the day, the small herd of elephant, at a run, exploded over the rise – tumbling down to water, scattering all before them – I was very glad I'd crossed over to the other side. They'd have come right over the top of me otherwise.

Loose-limbed in their excitement, ears flapping, trunks waving, the elephants rushed down to the pool. Soon, all were siphoning up their first trunkfuls of water to release into parched throats. They entered deeper into the grass- and weed-covered pool, and I knew that they could reach me easily. But I sat tight, watching and working the cameras as, absorbed in their own delight, they partook of the life-giving water.

Then, they were mud-bathing, the calves down and rolling. Mud squirted from one trunk after another, and a glorious time was had by all. Underfoot, the little ones lay and squirmed: ecstatic stuff, mud . . . as every child knows. Or should.

Soon, all were siphoning up their first trunkfuls . . .

. . . to release into parched throats.

They entered deeper . . .

Underfoot, the little ones lay and squirmed . . .

13

Ecstatic stuff, mud . . .

Yet death was to draw even nearer, perhaps, before that first day was out. I'd walked back in the mid-afternoon heat to the forward control Land Rover that was my home-away-from-home; dowsing my head with water, I'd fallen on the bed and slept. Half an hour later, drenched in sweat, I awoke, sat up – and a bee buzzed loudly in front of my face. I blew it away and, instead of leaving, it flew in and stung me right on the tip of my nose.

Then I made the day's next mistake. Still groggy with sleep, I killed it. Others began pouring in through the open door of the vehicle. They, too, began to attack; and battle was joined.

Immediately, I made another mistake. Grabbing a tin of insect-repellent, I sprayed it all about, infuriating the rapidly-growing number of bees even more.

'No!' I shouted out loud. 'This can't be happening!'

Bees were in my hair, stinging my ears; they stung my arms, my bare torso, front and back, my legs and, each second, more and more were flying into the enclosed space of the vehicle's interior through that open side door. I'd have to close it, I realised.

Braving the storm of angry avengers, meeting the tiny, buzzing bodies in the opening, I jumped down, grabbed the handle of the door and pulled. It came off in my hand! Throwing the handle down, I grasped the door, swung it and jumped in again ahead of the weight of it. Then I closed the windows and began killing.

Soon, bees filled the cab and began to find their way in through a small opening above the second door, behind the driving and living areas of the vehicle. This advance party – fortunately, it was not a real swarm – was really angry now. I had to pack pillows and a blanket into the space above the door to be safe from them at last.

By the time I had killed all the bees inside, I had taken – so far as I could count – not less than thirty stings. It had all happened in a very few seconds, but I was considerably shaken by the experience. Those little, black barbs that I could see, I removed – trying to leave the sacs intact – with a fingernail. Then I took an antihistamine.

Shaking, wet with perspiration, I bathed myself, then sat listening to the sound of angry bees outside this oven-hot prison that my vehicle had become. It took quite a while for the buzzing to diminish and I thought it time to get into the front and drive back to camp.

More shocked by the savagery of the attack than the pain itself, I put my hand out to the door – no handle. And the other door was locked. The keys? They were outside, hanging in the lock of the door missing its inside handle. My home-become-prison was now a trap!

Laughing at the ridiculousness of the situation – frustrated, too – I speculated, "Take out a window? And if the party comes back?' Better to wait, I decided.

So there I sat until, a while later, a vehicle came by. Opening the window and poking my head through, I said, 'Would you mind unlocking my side door?'

I'd already met the family, fortunately.

As the man switched off and started to get out of his own vehicle, I added, 'Be careful. There are bees about.'

'Don't worry,' he replied. 'They never sting me.'

But he too was stung before he could get around to the other side of the Land Rover.

Zebras and impalas . . .

The enforced proximities of a city, I am – at best – able to endure. So, recording the life of the animals that, daily – some of them twice a day – visited the pool allowed me, once again, to revel in the aloneness and the space. I was the only human there; and 'loneliness' in the presence of so much life is, I have found, entirely bearable.

These were the dying days of the year. But before a new season's rainfall began, the animals' desperation would increase, as intense heat added its contribution to the effects of the previous season's drought. The situation soon had my full attention. Working to capture the nuances of behaviour requires great concentration – bee stings notwithstanding.

Zebras and impalas in herds coming across the floodplain's broad expanse; shier animals – kudus, bushbuck and the rare nyalas – emerging from the thick bush on the south side: Chine Pool was a hive of activity. And, most of the time, it was of an entirely peaceful kind. Even in times of stress, life goes on. My self-appointed task was to watch and record it.

When the kudus arrive, one cow drinks near an impala doe.

The troop of baboons makes a leisurely way . . .

The troop of baboons makes a leisurely way down to drink; and they rest too, beside the water's edge. They also play the spectators' game – all but the youngsters who soon are gambolling about. Some adults begin picking and eating tasty bits of the greenery growing on top of the water, while others – backs to the area of potential danger – sit and relax, confident that one of their number will warn of any impending threat.

Suddenly, a skirmish sends a young baboon hurtling towards me, to scramble up a tree almost above my head. A large male leaps after him, driving the adolescent to an ever more precarious position, until he hangs screaming beneath this tormentor – who, to make matters worse, rhythmically shakes the branch by bouncing up and down on it, driving his lesson home. Punishment over, he climbs down and allows the chastened youngster to scramble towards safety, then flee in the direction of the departing troop. At his leisure, the dominant male follows after.

When the kudus arrive, one cow drinks near an impala doe. In the middle distance, a fine eland walks, oxpeckers riding on his neck and back. Will he come to the water? No. Threading his way through the troops of baboons, he continues on behind me.

Impalas drinking, baboons passing, nyalas joining the other animals . . . now a bushbuck doe takes centre stage, dipping her head to water. Four species in one picture! I am exultant. It really is a bonus, when one is able to illustrate the differences between three kinds of antelope in a single photograph.

Four species in one picture!

In the middle distance, a fine eland walks . . .

When the nyala female led her baby away, the little one was accompanied by the bushbuck doe.

The dangers of that first day had, I realised, been entirely self-induced. Of course, I should have known better. So soon, one loses one's sense of perspective in the competitive atmosphere of the city. But, if you forget your lessons, the African bush will certainly teach you once again. And the first thing to learn is *respect*. After that close encounter with the elephant cow and calf, whenever potentially dangerous animals drew near, I never hesitated to let them know – in good time – that I was there.

Now, I decided, I would not sit in concealment whenever I settled down beside Chine Pool either. On the next visit, I sat below the level of the bank. Yes, breaking my silhouette. And I sat – of course – in the shade, for more than one reason. Animals, particularly antelopes, would be less likely to see me from a distance then. And I would always try to remain motionless as they drew near.

Thereafter, when they did hear the sound of the camera or the motor drive – when it was working – provided I stayed still, more often than not they did not react violently, leaping away, but stared, even came forward . . . and, satisfied that I represented no threat, drank. Only occasionally did the attentions of a tsetse fly force an involuntary movement, accompanied – sometimes – by a muttered imprecation!

When the nyala female led her baby away, the little one was accompanied by the bushbuck doe. Suddenly, life took on another dimension: a large elephant bull had silently come up behind me! Moving around, down, he vigorously began the bathing ritual. Though he was a fair way off, I was grateful the zoom lens allowed a proximity that, today, my heart would not have permitted. Only after his departure did it slowly return to an acceptable pace of measuring time's passing.

A zebra family came down in the elephant's wake; and I was thrilled that these nervous and excitable creatures chose to drink so close to me.

This is as good a time as any, perhaps, to explain another aspect of the way I've come to work. I don't manufacture situations. If a fish eagle sits in a tree and I want a flight picture, I won't disturb him in order to get it. Only when he seems ready to fly – they often defecate just before launching – will I train the lens upon him. Purist, you might say.

But the rewards of this attitude, though subtle, are many. Try it, and you'll discover this is a key to becoming one with the wild . . . and with creatures who, then, are not so wild, after all. And, always, I've wanted to capture each situation before me *as it is,* without preconceptions or any heightening of one or other aspect of the whole.

A red-billed oxpecker clinging to his neck, another riding on his back . . .

Three thousand or more impalas, I estimated, were drinking at the pool each day. Sometimes, from one end to the other – a distance of several hundred metres – the water's edge would be occupied. By contrast, the bushbuck came singly, or in pairs, picking their way out of the undergrowth and tentatively approaching the poolside. Baboons, an African fish eagle, elephants (again), zebras, warthogs and kudus – ears turning every which way – they came.

Kudus are my favourite antelope species: the grace of their movement is, I find, mesmerising – so much so that I forget to take pictures. But I never knew what species to expect next; and this fact served only to heighten my anticipation. Seldom was I disappointed: a great white egret, eland –

always passing, usually sporting red-billed oxpeckers – and, of course, the nyalas. If Chine Pool has a claim to fame, it has been earned by sightings of the nyalas that come to drink here.

Kudu and nyala at the poolside together: what a pleasure! Young bulls, both of them; and when the kudu began to dig his horns into the mud, the nyala's drink was interrupted. Nervously, he started away.

A red-billed oxpecker clinging to his neck, another riding on his back, a fine impala ram approaches. Sometimes, the oxpeckers will alight and drink, too.

Baboons, feeding; an Egyptian goose brakeing as he comes in to land; the panic, as impalas flee unnecessarily – a day's activities are endlessly varied.

Kudus and nyala at the poolside together.

Baboons, feeding; an Egyptian goose brakeing . . .

I'd found the door handle again on the morning after the incident of the bees, but parked in a different place just to be on the safe side. Elephants and bees: between them, these two species had certainly ensured that my regular visits to Chine Pool started 'with a bang'. The stings were not particularly painful but when my body temperature rose, the residual irritation – principally an itch – grew to be uncomfortable. I continued to take the antihistamines, two and then three a day, yet the swellings remained. So several visits to the pool were shortened; I arrived later, or left earlier.

Superficially, one might think that sitting beside the same pool, day after day, would be boring. But 'boring' is a word, I've found, that doesn't apply to natural situations. Once one begins to move – both outwardly and within – at the pace of whatever is happening about one, the word loses its meaning. And, while the concentrations of impalas remained dense, even increased, always there was something *different* happening – like watching kudu and an nyala together, for instance. How often does not get such an opportunity?

. . . the carcase of a hyena, lying there
. . . now up on its feet.

When, after an absence of several days, I made the usual cautious approach to Chine Pool, it was to find what I took, at first, to be the carcase of a hyena lying there. Sobered by the sight, I nevertheless settled down to begin another day's participation in the life of the pool with spirits high. The effect of the bee stings, by now, had worn off.

And so were the zebras.

. . . her curiosity about this strange creature.

A group of kudu cows . . .

It was still early in the morning, and the cocky young warthog that trotted down for a drink before breakfast cast a long shadow. As I opened my tin of grapefruit, a lilac-breasted roller screeched overhead, then sat on a nearby branch watching as I spooned the sections, one by one, into my mouth. Tipping the tin up, I drank the last of the juice: breakfast enough for me.

Chine Pool was shrinking fast; but the numbers of animals coming to drink here had not diminished at all. Impalas came and went, then a group of kudu cows joined the congregation. Not without a start or two, I regret to say; for the six cows and two half-grown calves were wary. Then I realised what had caused their premature exodus. It was the 'dead' hyena, now up on its feet. Slowly, it moved that emaciated body off into the bush.

When the hyena had gone, and before the next antelopes arrived, I was able to pay some attention to the bird life. An African jacana came visiting, stretching long legs and placing those widely-spread claws down on the nearby greenery. But the kudus were soon back, ears and eyes active as they approached the pool once more. This time, a young bull accompanied them, coming to stand like a rock in his stillness, before condescending to drop his nose to the water. The females still milled about, but he drank his fill now, allowing them to take their turn at the watcher's role.

Delicately, a bushbuck doe made her appearance, as if too shy to join the swelling numbers. Then, a tawny eagle flew the length of the pool.

'As if counting,' I said to myself, 'to make sure everyone was there.'

Well, *I* was there. And so were the zebras. On this occasion, they walked down behind me, and drank to my right, heads all down in a line, adding a final touch to their joined patterns' shimmering symmetry. But when, startled, they sprang away, it was in all directions.

Now, a kudu cow – oxpeckers flying – broke from the hold of the muddy pool to stand again, staring, once she had reached the safety of firm ground. Wet mud reached up those thin legs to the knees, and the big ears continued semaphoring even after she'd satisfied her curiosity about this strange creature with the noisy object that he kept lifting up in front of his nose.

Wading into the mud to reach cleaner water, the kudu's sisters drank. Then, thirst quenched, they lifted their legs from the clinging, squelching mud, gratefully setting those sharp hooves upon the hard standing again.

'Time for me, too,' I thought. So, I also took a deep, long draught of thirst-quenching liquid – though in my case it was lukewarm coffee. It's important to keep the level of one's fluids up.

An nyala doe surprised me by approaching on my right to drink where the zebras had stood. She was joined by a companion and together they took what they'd come for – a long, satisfying drink of reasonably clean water. Obviously, the far side of the pool was becoming difficult for them: soft mud, churned by the many hooves, now bordered the firmer ground, rather than weed-covered water.

Later, across the pool, impalas were massing, and a big male baboon sat in their midst. Then an impala ram walked right up to me . . . so close, I could not believe it! What, five metres? One knows what a privilege it is just to be alive, on occasions like these.

Time passed, almost every moment of it filled with incidents worthy of attention. In the distance, in the haze, yet another herd of impalas was approaching. Truly, their numbers seemed endless today.

And so the crowding of bodies about me continued.

Then, an impala ram walked right up . . .

Though I arrived later the next morning, the emaciated hyena was there again. Obviously, it was separated from the pack and too weak to kill on its own. How it continued to survive, I had no idea.

My idle speculations ceased – abruptly – on the arrival of another visitor. Elephants approach so silently; without warning, there he was, taking the final steps to begin, immediately, the business of cooling his body. A massive bull with short, thick tusks – one of them broken. He must have been very hot to bathe before drinking. And, twenty metres away, I clung to my seat and wondered at my audacity. (Yes, I was about to make another mistake.)

Swish went the trunk, and plop-plop the muddy water rained down upon his back. Soon, the head and ears, the upper portion of his body were wet and black, and he began to advance, looking for a cleaner place from which to drink. It was time to make my presence known.

When I stood up in front of him and spoke, inevitably – I suppose – the mock charge took place. Ears out, head up high, advancing a few swift paces, he swung his trunk. Camera lens zoomed right back, although the light was behind him, I took the picture.

But I had denied him his drink; and called his bluff, besides. Turning away, he mounted the bank, then halted beside a tree to glare angrily down at me. I carried on talking, expressing regret at disturbing him, and the elephant made as if to leave.

But, just as I was beginning to think it was all over, he turned and came again. A full-blooded charge this was, with the scream thrown in – a devastating noise, at that range. As the huge beast loomed up high, I had no choice but to stand and take it.

Somehow, I took the photograph, too. (Later, I was to think, 'That's going to be a great picture.' It probably was; when the rolls of film were returned from Switzerland, where they were processed, it was missing.)

When the bull turned away at last and began to retreat, I retaliated – the only time I've ever done so with an elephant – and shouted, 'That really wasn't necessary, you know!'

Somehow, I felt my own rights had been violated in those moments: that I, too, was entitled to a place beside Chine Pool.

So, without getting his drink, the large bull left the pool . . . and the small, quivering being who had denied him his privileges.

'A baboon would have moved out of his way,' I thought later. Much later.

Next morning, it was the buffalos turn.

Next morning, it was the buffalos' turn. Hardly had I settled down than, in the far distance, I saw the herd coming; early morning light, haze and dust combined to add beauty to the scene. Through the impalas, the leading animal advanced and, heads low, the rest followed after. It was a breathtaking sight; even the little billows of dust rising from the walking buffalos' hooves looked beautiful.

In leisurely fashion, the small herd angled down and around the pool to the far side. Baboons watched their progress with interest and, deferentially, the impalas gave way. Stretched out in a line becoming longer now as the leading animals neared the water, the buffalos came. There were calves among them, I noticed, and the largest bull was not the leading animal. Giving way, a few of

the impalas were forced to scramble across the drying mud, but most had already wandered off. Steadily, the buffalos approached the poolside, opposite where I sat.

But now the big bull halted, oxpeckers peering over his neck and back, to stare fixedly in my direction. The broad curve of his horns glinted in the sunlight. Would they panic and flee? No, they were entering the water, sinking deeply into the mud and, this time, the bull was one of the first. Oxpeckers shifted to sit on the bosses of horns as the buffalos, belly-deep in the muddy water, drank. The far edge of the pool was being thoroughly churned by the hooves of the herd; it would mean added difficulty, in days to come, for the sensitive nyalas and little bushbuck, I knew.

In leisurely fashion, the small herd . . .

Once more, the impalas drew near, hesitating as they veered around the now still form.

Finally, as peacefully as they had come, the herd left. And life returned once more to normal for the many antelopes about the pool. Spreading out, the troop of baboons began to pick at the weeds. A flock of guineafowl clucked their way down to the edge at the eastern end. Impalas came and went, came and went, as usual springing away at the slightest — sometimes imagined – disturbance, stampeding if the ripples of panic spread far enough. A squacco heron stepped up, as if to make my acquaintance.

Then a delightful bushbuck doe came walking by. Straight towards me, she headed . . . and she had seen me, too. Yet, curious, she lifted one foot after another and came on, first one ear laid back and then the other, shiny black nose held high. I was entranced.

Something startled her; incredibly swiftly, she wheeled about and bounded to the nearest thicket. Had it been the eagle circling overhead? Then, I saw . . . the hyena. Slowly, painfully, it was leaving the rim of the undergrowth further along the pool, heading down the slope towards the water's edge. Such a tragic sight; my heart went out to it.

The emaciated creature did not make it to the poolside. Instead, full in the sunlight, it lay in a hollow of the dry, cracked mud, right in the path of the animals' approach. When the head flopped down, I knew it had come to die. And so the hyena's plight came, for me, to symbolise what was happening here, at Chine Pool.

Tragedy lay beneath the beauty that enthralled. In this September heat, drought was taking its inevitable toll, and many were the animals that would be likely to give their lives up to it before the rains came. So did my mood shift from delighted, appreciative participation to sober, introspective meditation about the fate of the hyena.

Once more, the impalas drew near, hesitating as they veered around the now still form. The hyena's eye was open, receiving the full glare of the sun's light; in minutes, the retina would burn, I was certain. It was surely the end.

Resisting the urge to walk across, I kept my position. The bushbuck doe crept out from her hiding place and came once again to the water's edge. There, one forehoof raised, she stood looking in the hyena's direction. A few paces on, she turned for another stare. Then she walked along the greenery's edge, searching for a place to stand and drink . . . but always pausing to turn, again and again, giving attention to the motionless form.

When, finally, she drank, she was subjected to the malicious attention of an impala ram; spitefully, he dipped his head and poked her rump with a tip of his horn, and the little bushbuck sprang away from the water's edge once more!

In the distance, a kudu bull was steadily moving nearer, impalas trailing in his wake. Then the hyena rolled over . . . and the nearer antelopes scattered and ran. How tenacious life is! But this poor creature's time was about to be ended at last, and in a way that enraged me.

Emerging from the thick brush, chasing all that remained near the pool before them, two Australian tourists walked up to the hyena, looked at it, then one beat it to death with bits of log that fragmented as he struck the animal. He was certainly unaware I had photographed the deed, committed no doubt out of pity – did he know it was enough to get him thrown out of the park if reported? Off they went, in the direction from which the kudu had been approaching, to return half an hour later, disturbing the life of the pool once more. And still they didn't see me, sitting there.

. . . beat it to death with bits of log that fragmented as he struck the animal.

It was a while before things settled down after this disruption. But finally the baboons came, and a pair of kudu cows took the place of the bull. The pattern of comings and goings re-established itself, and I was once more able to observe peacefully the continuing life of the pool.

The baboons were moving about the water now, drinking and resting, beginning to feed on the weed. Skittish and awkward, a kudu calf stepped upon the drying mud surface. Then the nyalas came.

Zebras took fright before they reached the pool-side, cantering away again. But the nyalas remained, and drank . . . not without nervousness, however. When the bull dug at the turf with those fine horns of his, a clod adhered; he interrupted his activities to shake it off. Thirst not yet quenched, he drank a second time, while his companions began their trek back towards the safety of the bush.

. . . a kudu calf stepped upon the drying mud surface.

But, the nyalas remained, and drank . . . not without nervousness, however.

Next, on the far side, a bushbuck ram.

Next, on the far side, a bushbuck ram; was it the same animal I had seen before? I had not yet got to know the animals well enough to be sure. After drinking, he too sprang away, soon disappearing from sight.

An impala doe watched me curiously, while an oxpecker seemed to whisper in her ear.

'It's all right, he's harmless,' I thought the words for the little bird.

Then, as the impalas closer at hand spread out and began to drink without disturbance, I turned to capture the scene with a wide-angle shot.

A young nyala bull walked right úp to the carcase of the hyena now, surprising me with this show of audacity. When he left the pool, a young kudu bull was passing in the opposite direction, so I was given another chance to photograph my two favourite antelope species together.

Near and far, there were animals, again, everywhere: life – prolific – defying the drought. Less than ten paces away, an impala doe stood her ground, staring. And when, undisturbed, she took her departure, I watched the space being filled by zebras. Right beside me, they came to stand and drink, attention given to the muddy water. Had they learned to recognise me, and know that I posed no threat?

Slowly, the shadows crept eastward, as the turnabout continued. A warthog took the zebras' place, drinking, then lolling in the mud contentedly. But he kept a sharp eye on my still form before rising and, thoroughly mud-covered, making off again.

Another member of his crinkly clan soon took his place. Muddy bellied, he too left, to be replaced by a third. Only when his curiosity had been completely satisfied did this last individual settle down to drink. Different behaviour shown by various members of the same species: it all added flavour to the continuing activity.

Next came another contingent of impalas, led by a boldly striding ram, coat resplendent in the afternoon sunlight. A doe, jockey twins perched on her back, looked briefly in my direction before attending to matters of greater relevance. Then a fine kudu bull strode up, walking straight towards the sun.

A young nyala bull walked right up to the carcase . . .

When he left, a young kudu bull was passing . . .

A warthog took the zebra's place . . .

Only when his curiosity had been completely satisfied . . .

. . . jockey twins perched on her back.

. . . walking straight towards the sun.

. . . he assumed the classic pose. Then, past an approaching dog baboon . . .

. . . the two kudu bulls joined the baboons.

My breathing rate is always affected when I watch these magnificent creatures. Nonchalant in his majesty, the bull traversed the pool opposite, pausing now and then to survey his surroundings. At last, the camera's small noise – no motor drive – attracted his attention, and he assumed the classic pose. Then, past an approaching dog baboon, he continued his unhurried pacing.

I had been so absorbed by this king of the bush that the presence of one of his lieutenants, when I saw him, took me by surprise. He, too, was favouring me with undivided attention: frozen, I sat. At last, the two kudu bulls joined the baboons who were feeding on the pool's greenery. Together they drank and, politely, as if unaware – but on as *if* unaware – the baboons ignored them.

That evening, the buffalos returned; from the same direction as they had come in the morning, the little herd trailed down towards Chine Pool in the fading light. When, noses active, the leading animals stopped before the carcase of the hyena, I wasn't surprised. But when, a few minutes later, an elephant suddenly appeared above the scene, he startled all of us! Already deep in the mud, a buffalo calf was left behind in the wake of the herd's precipitous departure; scrabbling free, he raced to join them.

Tails high, the buffalos stampeded after the already distant kudus, while the baboons sat and enjoyed the evening's entertainment. The little herd split; around the bushes and up towards the rim, some of the buffalos charged, leaving a pall of dust; the rest slowed their mad retreat and, stopping, turned to face the way they had come.

Like the gentleman he was, the elephant waited until all pandemonium had ceased, delicately probing the dry brush beside him with the tip of his trunk. Then, as if released, he brought that tremendous shadow of his down to the pool. Once there, he drank and bathed, then ambled along. And the hindmost buffalos returned.

Slowly, these great beasts drew near to one another – and the dead hyena, like a victim in no-man's land, lay motionless between them.

When the nearest pair of buffalos, heads down, were sniffing to investigate the carcase, the elephant bull turned and – as the saying goes in these parts – 'gave them a rev'. But there was no confrontation; the elephant turned away and, stepping over the erosion cracks, passed opposite me once more.

Suddenly, he was running; tail curling, stepping high, he departed the scene. Why? I don't know. Perhaps, wafted on a little gust of evening wind, the hyena's smell had distressed him.

Surprisingly, there were no vultures about when I arrived at Chine Pool next morning – I'd expected them to be feasting on the dead hyena. A pair of magnificently adorned kudu bulls soon joined the baboons, the impalas and me. Even the baboons stared at those curving appendages, as if aware of their splendour! But the preoccupation with water continued, and the baboons and impalas were soon thoroughly intermingled. And yet, before long, the inevitable impala stampede occurred. So I settled down to another day of watching and photographing.

Sometimes, the camera captures sights that the eye fails to see . . . or perhaps that the memory fails to retain. Whenever another impala sprang high, I would try to time the shutter's release with the peak of the leap. Far too often, I missed, of course; but there's a lot of fun to be had in the trying!

The kudu bulls had lingered, and a number of cows had joined them by now. Craning their necks forward, ears back, they drank. Heads swivelled, water dribbled from mouths, and the black horns shone in the sunlight. Then the two males left the females, still in the water; one behind the other, they headed off towards the north-east. One of the cows sank knee-deep in the mud – front legs, then back – as she struggled across the narrow strip of soft earth to join her friends. And, nearer to hand, a baboon munching on a bite of greenery watched, too.

More kudus arrived and drank close to where I sat. One female was literally festooned with oxpeckers.

Fat zebras, startled by something I couldn't see, turned from the water and galloped off. Belatedly, I realised what all the commotion was about: an elephant . . . naturally, an elephant had arrived. Confidently, he made his way down past the fallen tree where I'd sat that first morning. Slapping himself with mud a few times, he continued around the eastern end of the pool, leaving the impalas – and me – more or less undisturbed. Perhaps he was heading for cleaner water.

Now, it was that incredible nyala bull's turn. Head down, he strode thirstily across in front of me, glancing in my direction only briefly. Almost immediately, he was drinking, and I watched the hollow behind his ribs beginning to fill. When, finally, he lifted his head, his tongue continued to lick; then he moved a few paces down, and – white hairs showing clearly on his back – drank once more. Without attacking the mud with his horns this time, he turned and left. And I sat, yet again filled with awe at the beauty of this creature who, by his very presence – so brief – had enriched my day.

Baboons foraged to my left, to my right. Wherever they could find acceptable water and ground fit to stand upon, the impalas drank. And, on both sides, the kudus came down from behind and quenched that inevitable thirst. They were nervous, but when they moved away from the water, it was towards me: obviously, I was not the cause of their nervousness.

Some of the younger baboons had climbed up on top of low, dry bushes, the better to survey their surroundings. But not for that reason only; soon, they were playing. My original viewing place was also occupied now: perhaps the baboons sitting there were more used to elephants than I was!

Nearer by, a youngster was investigating his penis and, shocking those vestiges of Victorian attitudes I still harbour within, put his mouth down to the head of the pink organ. Perhaps he was only cleaning it.

When a western banded snake eagle, flying low and straight, came past, I was able to train and focus the lens rapidly enough, for once; the identification of this seldom-seen raptor came later, of course.

No buffalos, today; no black rhinos . . . not even a vulture settling down on the carcase across the pool. It was smelling so much now that – even at this distance – I was wrinkling my nose.

A western banded snake eagle, flying low and straight.

A kudu cow was one of the animals to please next morning, so close did she drink. Zebras joined her, and the oxpeckers flew from one host to the other, until there were many birds clinging to the cow's neck, or riding up on her body. As she drank, a thirsty impala craned his neck forward and soon he was decorated with an oxpecker, too.

When the kudu walked off, I watched the zebras – normally so uneasy near water – drinking placidly beside me. Had they come to realise they were safer here, I wondered now? Even the oxpeckers, flying from one host to another, appeared to be indifferent to my presence. And oxpeckers are extremely alert, seldom tolerant, birds.

Head down, a bushbuck made her way steadily, step by step, towards the water. Ears back, she halted on the rim of the hard ground – before her, only a mud-broken surface, now – and stared at my still form.

'Don't be afraid.' I said it, softly but aloud this time.

And, moving on, she approached one of the Egyptian geese – no luck there – passed a long-tailed starling and continued her search. Ignoring her, a big male baboon walked by; and, when finally she drank, it was beside another of his ilk.

'Mission accomplished,' I breathed.

The great white egret had a sacred ibis for company, the next time I arrived at Chine Pool. And, as I settled in, a hamerkop flew by, to settle at the other end. Deciding he, too, needed a change of scenery the egret – neck drawn back – flew the same route. And I wondered whether the ibis would follow. But he was content to remain.

Doves in numbers were drinking, this morning – not the little green-spotted doves, whose whirring wings, as they settled in hundreds, added a new note to the tonal symphony in the afternoons, but laughing doves, Cape turtle-doves, even a green wood pigeon or two. Finally, the ibis did decide to join the egret. And, behind me, impalas moved.

Then, the nyala bull – neck stretched out as, thirstily, he gained the level ground and headed towards the one remaining safe drinking place on the far side – demanded attention. His forelegs sank down deeply; and, when the females arrived, that restless turnabout that I had come to know so well was soon in full swing.

. . . the little bushback doe appeared and looked uncertainly down upn the scene.

Hindquarters braced, he stood staring up over the rise . . .

Handsome in his prime, a bushbuck ram stood a little apart, watching. Baboons, too; and then the little bushbuck doe appeared and looked uncertainly down upon the scene.

Suddenly and inexplicably, panic struck; everyone cleared off, leaving me to my meditations.

The bushbuck ram was the first to reappear. Hindquarters braced, he stood staring up over the rise for quite a while. Even when he drew nearer, he continued to survey the surrounding area with extra care.

Only minutes later did he finally relax his guard and come on down. Though thirsty in that midmorning heat, once again he paused, directly opposite, the white on his throat showing clearly. Then, he gingerly stepped onto the mud; uncertainly, tail active, he stood. Impalas appeared and he sprang away, to stand looking over his shoulder. Back in my direction, he came; he'd decided it was not a safe place.

The bushbuck's coat shone as if it had been brushed when he walked by, once more, opposite me. Suddenly, he sprang away . . .

Another day: nibbling on a biscuit, I watched the procession of the animals. A bushbuck ram drank beside an nyala female; and another of these delicate creatures, leading a youngster, arrived. More females, and a second youngster, followed; and soon there were six nyala females and two young ones moving and turning, seeking a safe place at which to stand and drink together.

But the buffalo herd had ruined most of the far side of the pool for them. Only one place remained, where the sharp-hooved antelopes could find a comparatively secure purchase on hard ground and lower their heads to water. Restlessly – thirsty – they started and turned, offspring following mother; and,

before they could settle down at that one safe place, something really frightened them and the nyalas retreated to the safety of the bush once more.

Chine Pool had shrunk dramatically; clearly, it couldn't continue to function much longer as a watering place for the many animals visiting it. Water had become mud and, when a zebra tried to find liquid clean enough to drink, he was forced to wade right into the sticky stuff. All around the perimeter, the animals moved, reluctantly stepping on to the cracked and drying mud surface – hard on top, soft underneath – searching, searching for a place to drink.

Head back, resting . . .

At the eastern end of the pool, only a thin strip of muddy water remained, and here the impalas were competing for the meagre available space. I was watching them when I heard, directly across the pool from where I sat, two rifle shots fired.

'Not FN,' I thought. 'Not AK. Poachers?'

The sounds had been close together . . . and close, too.

On this day, I had been sitting with Charles Lewis and Fiona Wallace, holidaying in the park; breaking our own silence, we discussed the matter. They'd been about to leave anyway, and now they decided to return to their vehicle, parked about a kilometre away.

'Please report it,' I called after them, as they departed.

I was left wondering what had been going on in the thick bush opposite, as I waited for peace to settle about the pool. Not without nervousness, either, for a fierce battle with poachers who had come to kill and cut off the horns of the remaining black rhinos was but one of the many activities occupying staff in this National Park. And these poachers shoot – and are sometimes shot – on sight.

Before the animals began returning, however, the question was answered. Out of the bush opposite came Rob Shattock – a safari operator, and another friend – together with some clients. They were carrying one of their number.

'Of course. Rob's .404,' was my first thought; followed by, 'Something serious has happened.'

Moving toward my right, they came to a tree, and placed the injured person – a man, I saw – down beside it. By this time, I was up and moving, attracting Rob's attention.

'Can I help?' I called across the pool.

'Jesus, John. I was almost squashed by an elephant!' Rob replied when he saw me.

He asked me to fetch my Land Rover. I told him about the couple who had only recently left, saying their vehicle was parked much nearer than mine. Still carrying the rifle, he went after Charles and Fiona, running.

'I'll come over,' I said to his clients, beside the tree.

. . . tusked in the foot.

The man, I discovered when I reached them, had been tusked in the foot. Head back, resting against the bole of the tree, he sat with the injured foot up on a small carry-bag. He was pale with shock.

Yet, when I asked, 'Can I take your photograph?' he was able to smile, and reply.

'Sure. Send me one.'

There was surprisingly little blood. Sitting beside Mr Rade, as I learned later his name was, I explained where Rob had gone, assuring him the vehicle wouldn't be long in arriving. Then I discovered an elephant's long hair on the injured leg, and gave it to him. Silently, Mr Rade's companions sat about us . . . no doubt vividly reliving the intensity of their experience.

Soon Rob returned, leading the vehicle over the broken ground. He helped the others lift Mr Rade, and the injured man was eased through the sliding door of the van. Once he was settled inside, one of the ladies gave him a little water to drink. Hands together, he lay calmly while the final preparations before departure were made. A concerned Rob Shattock sat beside the client whose life he had saved.

He helped the others lift . . .

. . . the injured man was eased.

. . . through the sliding door of the van.

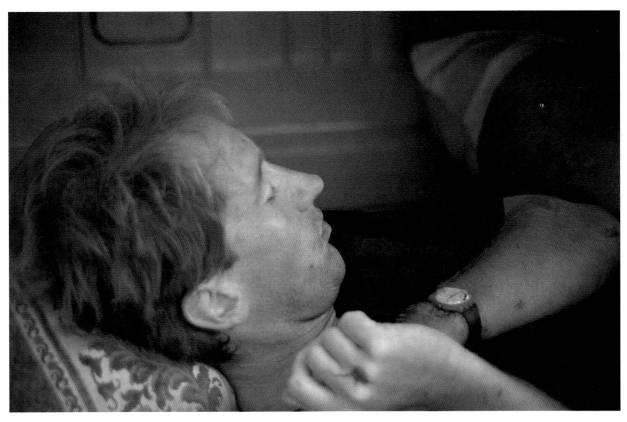

Hands together, he lay calmly . . .

Later, I was told the whole story. Rob had taken his clients into the brush south of Chine Pool to look for – of all things – nyala. Hearing the trumpeting of an elephant and the breaking of branches, he'd tried to lead them across-wind, positioning himself in front of the only decent tree in the vicinity – himself in front, clients behind – while the enraged animal continued to advance.

'I threw my hat,' he told me. 'I didn't want to shoot her.'

And, as he said it, the appeal for understanding was there in his eyes.

It must have happened very quickly. The cow elephant pinned Rob to the tree – the tusk going past his ear, with her head striking his head – throwing him back . . . . Fortunately, the bole of the tree was half hollow: only this fact saved Rob from death or serious injury.

After trying to crush Rob, the elephant moved around the tree towards the clients and, following,

Rob saw Mr Rade beneath her. The cow was about to kneel on her victim, and all he could think, Rob told me, was, 'I mustn't kill her. I mustn't kill her.'

If he had, she would have fallen on Mr Rade.

So, Rob aimed high. Firing from a distance of only a few paces, he shot the elephant in the temple. The impact of the bullet threw the animal backwards and sideways, so that her forehead was presented to Rob's view. Again, he fired high; and, once more, the animal was thrown back . . . now, Rob was able to run in and drag Mr Rade back to the tree.

Then, they heard the other elephants coming. The cow, still on her feet, had turned away to join them. So they picked Mr Rade up, and ran with him towards Chine Pool.

Afterwards, Rob said, he asked them how far they thought they had carried Mr Rade. Between 80 and 120 metres, the estimates varied. The distance, as it was paced out later in the day, was 550 metres.

This is the report Rob Shattock wrote for the Parks Board. When he gave me permission to use it here, he wrote on the back of the photocopy the following words:

> Dear John
>
> You saw the results – by being in the 'right place at the right time' - something that happens once or twice in a lifetime. Once is enough!
>
> Thank you for your help.
>
> Rob

Rob Shattock Safaris (Pvt) Ltd
No 17 Mucharara Crescent
Kariba. Tel: 2744. Telex 4028
Friday 25.9.1987

The Director
National Parks & Wildlife
C/o The Warden
Mana Pools National Park

Ref. Elephant Cow Accident Report.

Dear Sir,

Herewith report of accident on Friday 25/9/87 at approximately 9.30 am at Loc QN 548582 to R. P. Shattock (guide) and member of party Mr Kees Rade – Austrian, 33 years of Amsterdam, Holland.

Whilst walking northwards towards Chine Pool, with steady wind blowing across from east to west, I heard an elephant trumpet a good distance away to the west of us. Walking slowly looking for nyala I heard the trumpet again and dead vegetation breaking. Realising that it was possibly our wind and scent – the clients were instructed to run north with me on the game trail to get across the wind lie. Seeing only a single large tree to take cover in a safe place, the elephant continued crashing through the dead vegetation towards the direction of where we had been – about 30–50 metres south. Standing at the tree with a good view behind me and the party in safety behind me, I saw a cow elephant about 50 metres away going first from the west, then suddenly change on our tracks and run towards us. Realising that the cow was small and serious I shouted, whistled and screamed at her. She persisted in charging and then folded her trunk inwards at about 15 paces. Loading my rifle .404 with solid, I threw my hat at her and hoped she would stop still shouting at her. She slewed past the tree squashing me against the large tree and then spun around the tree where the clients were. Mr Rade was dragged away by the cow as I came around after her. As she was trying to tusk him underneath her I fired at point blank range high frontal into her head – this knocked her backwards and sideways – where I fired a second high temple shot which pushed her backwards again from Mr Rade who was now no longer beneath the elephant. Blood squirted from the wounds to her head and I ran and grabbed Mr Rade and pulled him to the tree. The other elephants were now approaching 7/8/9. The cow then staggered off going southwards. We then carried the injured to Chine.

Checking for injuries, it was discovered that the cow had put a tusk into the inside sole of Mr Rade's left foot. Not damaging any bones. There was no bleeding. Arriving at Chine Pool I ran to get assistance from a Mr/Mrs Lewis who had a vehicle about a kilometre away on the Sapi road. The injured was bandaged and taken immediately to the main camp site where a doctor was known to be adjacent to our site. First aid was given and I reported the accident to the senior ranger Mr M. Brightman and returned with further first aid equipment and Dr L. Gibson. The injured was then taken to Kariba Hospital.

Herewith plan of site of accident as a result of returning to scene to do follow up with Parks staff.

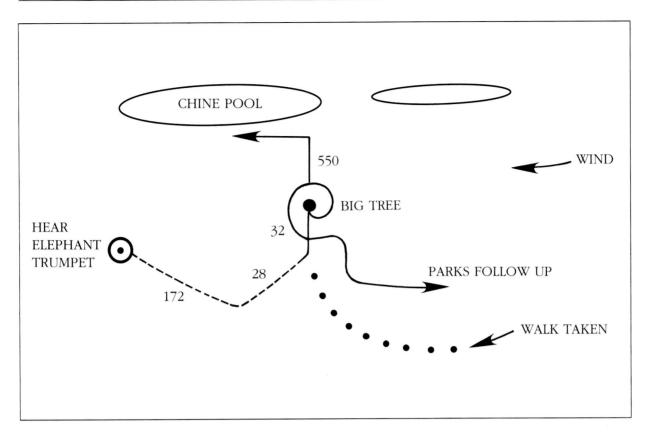

Conclusion: A most fortunate experience having a firearm for safety reasons, animals are under stress because of the shortage of food and access to concealed water at pans. Increased walking could also be a problem – through lack of knowledge and understanding of animal habits and feeding. Trusting this information will suffice. Extreme thanks for prompt action and follow up to Mr Brightman and his staff and medical team.

Sincerely

(signed) (signed)

After being flown to Kariba in a helicopter, Mr Rade – who had suffered severed tendons in the heel – received surgical attention in Harare. Within weeks, he was walking again.

'And without a limp,' Rob told me, when we sat sharing his experience all over again, and drinking coffee together. 'He says he's coming back next year.'

Three incidents in ten days – and this had been the third. And we were not even into 'suicide month ' – October – yet. Two elephants and a buffalo; and, after the first incident, I'd doubled my 'safe' distances while walking. Clearly, the animals were now under great stress. Back beside the pool, I thought about elephants.

This latest incident – where the cow came in unprovoked, on scent alone, and not with any 'mock' charge, either – proved that, even with all the care in the world, sooner or later your luck will run out.

As Rob's had done; thought not all of it, thank God!

'Ten out of ten for the way you handled it, Rob,' I thought to myself.

(That afternoon, he was still high on adrenalin.)

We humans, I meditated, after the others had left, tend to carry on regardless . . . not taking changing situations into account, not fully realising the implications – heat, the cumulative effects of the drought, waterholes drying, practically nothing to eat – and so we take the consequences. And, what about the changing situations in our own lives?

Again, the animals came. A baboon led the way; others followed and, soon, nyalas . . . the rare creatures Rob and his group had been scouring the bush to find. The pattern of the day's activities had returned to normal.

Impalas crowded the limited drinking places, and shining droplets of water flew when one slipped. Squawking as if to say, 'What, are you still here?' an Eqyptian goose, eyeing me, flew by. And then, nearer the still unoccupied western end, the pair of geese – and another – after wheeling and turning, landed near a pair of saddlebilled storks.

The congregating impalas were definitely thinner. They drank reluctantly, for it was more mud than water the pool offered now. When a doe lifted her head, searching the area behind her, the dark deposit on her muzzle showed clearly.

They seemed to have lost all fear of me. Mouthing her tongue, this girl stood close for quite a while before, quietly, moving away. And my heart, too, was quietened as, again, I became conscious of the privilege accorded by this shared proximity.

Further off, the thirsty drinking, the unexpected penetration of a sharp hoof – the falling – continued. And the concentration of animals increased.

Incessantly, the impalas moved about me. When one fell, others would spring away . . . but only a few metres. No longer was there any headlong flight: the need for water had become too great for that. Often, I noticed, it was the younger animals that found themselves in trouble. And, through the haze, the sun continued to shine down upon the scene, burning hot – heating those thirsty bodies still further – but making the whole look beautiful.

Between them, an impala drank and, as usual, there was always one head lifted . . .

Not for the first time, I'd taken a break from my vigil beside Chine Pool and wandered further afield. Now, I was back. Guineafowl moved away from the water's edge as I drew near, and a goliath heron flew off. This disturbed the great white egret, who lifted himself up into the air, higher and higher, and – surprising me – settled on the tree above my head. It was a fine way for him to say, on behalf of the pool, 'Welcome'.

A little later, the nyalas arrived. Between them, an impala drank and, as usual, there was always at least one head lifted as look-out. They co-operated, these animals: even between species, the mutual support was there.

Soon, the impalas were drinking beside me again. Next, a new visitor; tongue flicking, a leguaan waddled down towards the pool. He found the place too crowded, I think, for when a bushbuck sprang in alarm and the impalas ran, he too turned and left.

Baboons joined the crowd and, near them, the bushbuck doe was able to trust herself to drink. Then, over the lip of high ground beyond the pool, the kudu cows appeared. A fine young bull, too, came down to take the bushbuck's place beside the feeding baboons. Something startled the bushbuck doe, however, and the bull sprang away in her wake.

. . . too nervous to try for water now.

Leaping and bounding, the kudu cows and calves followed after. But the young bull stopped before reaching the thickets above the pool, and this steadied the others. Wheeling and searching in all directions, they remained in view, until a further disturbance sent them off, in full flight, once again. I was left to set the camera down, and wait for the next bout of activity.

A bushbuck ram sought a place beside the broken line of the water's edge, and the female joined him: together, they drank. A little later, the kudu cows – without their male escort this time – came back, to make their way along that widening space between the shrinking pool and the higher ground above it. Still uncertain, they stood in a little group, clustered near to where the hyena had met its end. Eleven, I counted, including a full complement of youngsters. Back they turned, in my direction, walking . . . too nervous to try for water now.

Baboons joined me, and the impalas milled about, crowding the poolside. Almost immediately, a youngster was down, small, sharp hooves penetrating the drying surface of the mud, so that she struggled frantically to release her legs from the grip of the clinging softness beneath. As close as ever, they came to drink; and the light of the morning sun glinted off their thinning bodies and the muddied surface of the pool. Zebras followed; I zoomed the lens back even further to accommodate their larger frames in the viewfinder. Mud went spattering, as they fled the camera's small sound. But the impalas soon returned.

Lifting her hooves high, a female entered the muddy pool next to where I sat. Dipping her muzzle, she licked the surface, then turned, mouthing the mud on her tongue. It was obviously undrinkable. Carefully, she eased herself out again.

Warthogs found temporarily undisturbed places; and the zebras returned, stepping into an area where the green surface had not yet been churned into mud. Others followed and, again, the alarm of one led to a startled exit of the rest. A baboon turned to watch an impala struggling nearby.

. . . the alarm of one led to a startled exit of the rest.

And then I turned my attention, for the moment, from the drama and tensions of the mud to enjoy the placidity in a proud young kudu bull's approach. Straight in my direction he stared; satisfied, finally, he moved on again. A cow beside a second young bull shook the oxpeckers from her hide impatiently, and the birds – co-operating, for a change: there were many hosts in the vicinity – left her.

A baboon turned to watch an impala struggling nearby.

A cow beside a second young bull shook the oxpeckers from her hide impatiently . . .

Chine Pool was beginning to fail her many customers, now. Yet the animals continued to congregate: even in this depleted state, she represented their only source of life-giving water. It was a moving tableau, an all-absorbing scene, that I worked carefully to capture on film as well as I could. But I cannot put into words the heart-wrenching, almost breathless awareness it aroused in me.

Once more, the thirsty, mud-bespattered zebras were back. Sinking almost belly-deep into the mud, the stallion drank . . . drank mud, or tried to. First one place, then another, he sampled, easing himself through the clinging stickiness. Unhappy, he sprang powerfully away again.

The plight of the animals tore at my throat – yet, for the baboons, it seemed to be life as usual. The warthogs, too, looked comparatively undisturbed by the consistency of the fluid they consumed.

A thirsty young nyala bull claimed my camera's attention next: while – near and far – more warthogs slid into the mud and drank, he ran back and forth looking for a safe place, finally venturing across the cracked surface. It trapped him and, white tail-of-a-flag flying, he retreated towards higher ground.

The far side was unsafe, he'd decided; so he came around. Down the little slope beside me, he walked. A gust of wind blew, leaves flew – that was enough to make him wheel away. But not for long. Horns glinting in the sunlight, he stepped back towards where I sat. An nyala, so close: I could hardly believe it! Cautiously, he placed his forefeet into the soft, wet mud. They did not sink down. His muzzle dipped. At this distance, the large ear seemed almost transparent; tail held tightly between his legs, the young nyala bull drank.

Feeling safer now, he shifted his legs and turned his head, seeking a cleaner place. Then he moved backwards, lifting his hind legs high to free them. Hardly daring to move – to alter the zoom, even – I continued to work the camera. He heard it. Lifting his head, tongue out, he stared at me. And yet, he didn't spring away; he simply walked a little further off, to enter the muddy water and drink again. Truly, the young nyala had complimented me by drinking in such proximity.

Now, baboons and a bushbuck doe joined me. Then, after a while, it was the turn of a kudu calf to brave the dangers of the muddy pool.

The baboons were already there when I arrived next morning; obviously, they meant to make the most of the greenery atop the pool while it lasted. And a fine kudu bull was also down early, in position at the eastern end and drinking while the impalas moved all about him. How magnificently those spiralling horns shone in the morning light! Oxpeckers kept him company and, tail swinging, he strode off in the direction from which he had come.

Ahead and to my right, another fine kudu bull moved, then turned back when he found no suitable place. He also carried a full complement of oxpeckers as he stepped proudly out.

. . . a full complement of expeckers as he stepped proudly out.

Close by, a big dog baboon chewed meditatively on his bit of greenery. There was a sombre atmosphere about the place today. But the sunlight played on the animals' bodies, and little gusts of wind blew, ruffling the baboon's hair.

Some of the youngsters had begun to play now, and one climbed – king-of-the-castle style – upon a short log, the better to survey the activities of his minions. Over a soft area, a baboon leaped and, for a change, I caught the moment perfectly.

Guineafowl clucked and chattered their way down to the greenery's edge, while the great white egret stepped ever nearer. This was a large flock, and some of the birds sought the shade of dry, over-hanging bushes.

Ears back, a lovely bushbuck doe – head held low, black muzzle pointing her nose towards the smell of water – came close by me. Her coat gleamed and, hearing the sound of the camera, she halted momentarily, pricking her ears.

Nyalas, now, female and male; he with his head low, as if bowed by the weight of his horns, but in reality only because he was thirsty.

Over a soft area, a baboon leaped . . .

Ears back, a lovely bushbuck doe . . .

Nyalas, now, female and male . . .

Suddenly, there was pandemonium – an elephant had stopped on top of the ridge. Like a statue, the bull stood there; even his trunk was still. And the majesty of his presence spread the length and breadth of the pool.

At last, he came down, and the nearest baboons fled. This was a mature animal; possessively, he moved around the cracks, reconnoitring. I was glad to be on the far side!

Finally, he stepped into the soft mud; working with his trunk, swaying back and forth, he began the plastering process.

. . . even his trunk was still.

At last, he came down, and the nearest baboons fled.

Possessively, he moved around . . .

Swaying back and forth, he began the plastering process.

Beside me, a warthog entered the mud. Body stretched forward, one hind leg cocked, tail curling upward, he drank . . . if 'drank' is still the appropriate word. An nyala – another young bull – appeared; was it the same one that had favoured me with such close attention yesterday? If so, he hadn't learned his lesson; for, onto the treacherously soft, muddy surface he came.

Moving carefully, he reached the little, deep puddle where, earlier, a bushbuck had drunk, and lowered his muzzle there. Impalas followed; one slipped . . . startled, the nyala drew back. Soon, there were three antelopes with their forelegs deep – buttocks high – at that part of the pool, all trying to assuage their unforgiving thirst.

We were well into October now. The situation at Chine Pool had become critical. The plight of the animals was what I was forced to record, carefully working the camera and shooting a roll of faster film. Overcast skies promised an end to the drought, but made photography more difficult. Blacker than ever, the mud gleamed; and, more mud-bespattered than ever, the impalas struggled to escape its cloying grip, while yet they sought the little relief its moisture could give.

It was the inexperienced youngsters that most often fell. But even these occurrences did not alarm the others any longer, so frequent were they: no panic-stricken flights followed a fall. All were too concerned about their own, unremitting thirst. One by one, the animals would gather about a single depression in the mud, where a few precious drops of fluid remained. And when one female pulled her foreleg back from the mud's grip, it was released so violently that it hooked over another's neck.

A young male's foreleg stuck; trying to spring away, he went down again, and then a third time, before tremblingly regaining his feet. This young fellow fell so often that he finally drank lying down! When at last he arose to make his way safely to hard standing, I felt as if I wanted to cheer.

Only females were left. They seemed to be conferring above the little hole:

'No, nothing left here.'

As a pair of Egyptian geese wandered nearer, I recorded the grim details of the demise of Chine Pool.

High on the ridge on the far side, an nyala female stood.

'It's no use,' she seemed to be thinking; and, unable to bear the sight myself any longer, I left. Trumpeter hornbills flew overhead as I turned away.

It was the inexperienced youngsters that most often fell.

. . . a single depression in the mud.

. . . it was released so violently that it hooked over another's neck

Trying to spring away . . .

he went down again . . .   *. . . and then a third time.*

. . . he finally drank lying down.

. . . conferring above the little hole.

. . . a pair of Egyptian geese wandered nearer.

Twice more I returned to Chine Pool, but each time only briefly. On the first occasion, tracks through the mud and, where the sun had done its work, dry clay, baked and caked, met my eye. There were no animals. I didn't linger.

The second time, hamerkops entertained me briefly – whether with mating behaviour or simply displays of dominance, I was not sure. But the light showed their wing feathers most beautifully; and when, finally, most of them flew away, one remained. Was he drying his wings, or just taking the sun?

Animals, there were none. The pool, it seemed, had given up the ghost. But a flock of guineafowl spread themselves across the open ground, on the far side, moving nearer. Close to the bushes, they bunched up and, one by one, hopped over a log that lay in their path. Heads busy, clucking and chattering, they wandered along, finally making a strung-out way down to the edge of the dry pool.

I waited and, at last, four impalas came out of the bushes. One female, in particular, was pathetically thin, and bore markings of the mange that had begun to attack the body hair of some of the animals, exposing patches of bare skin. Many would die before the summer rains came. And there was no longer anything for them to drink here.

One female, in particular, was pathetically thin . . .